The Development of Mexican Identity

A Psychological Perspective

MANUEL ISAIAS LOPEZ, MD, PhD

Translation from Spanish by Alejandra Wortman, MD

<u>Front Cover</u>

"Excavation of Templo Mayor" (Greater Temple), which was the main temple in Tenochtitlán, dedicated to Huitzilopochtli (god of war) and Tláloc (god of rain). In 1521 it was destroyed by the Spaniards to build what later became Mexico City Metropolitan Cathedral (which is seen in the background). Image copyright © 2004 by David Lopez.

EDITORS' NOTE

The present text is a complete reproduction of the work as
conceived by the author in 1992. The division into chapters and
their titles is a later modification, and not of Dr. López' authorship.
In addition, all images were inserted *post hoc* to illustrate some of
the references made in the text.

David L. Lopez, MD and Alejandra Wortman, MD
November 2018, Greenwich, CT.

CONTENTS

AUTHOR'S NOTE

A shorter version of this manuscript was presented as the Keynote Address of the IX National Conference of the Mexican Association of Child Psychiatry (AMPI) in Guanajuato, Mexico on November 20, 1992. Before its presentation this text was discussed and enriched, during the class "Seminario de Desarrollo III" (on Adolescent Development) with the members of the 17th class of the Psychoanalytic Institute of the Mexican Psychoanalytic Association (APM).

1

GROUP IDENTITY IN ADOLESCENCE

Throughout childhood and adolescence, a wide array of phenomena come together to become part of what in Psychology we label *self-concept*: Gender, body image, personality traits, appearance, etc. There are various elements that form this structural integration. For instance, during childhood the parental concept of, and bearings towards, their child begin to shape the child's self-concept. During adolescence, all the subsequent cognitive, physical, and sexual modifications that occur to the adolescent compound it. All these elements coalesce into a mental representation, and are a part of the global emotional notion and awareness that the individual has of his or her self.

Among the multitude of elements of this structure, are also those derived from the group experience; in other words, the self-concept of the person within its group.

Freud studied the group phenomenon in 1930, and mainly considered it a means to protect man from nature and other humans. Erich Fromm (1947) described the group phenomenon as the gratification of a need particularly human. Blos, in 1962, studied the group phenomenon *vis à vis* its defensive role and as a fundamental part of the progressive-regressive journey of the adolescent. For my part (1990), I have studied the group phenomenon as a means to protect the individual from his own impulses. This mechanism gives rise to most myths and taboos, which are personal wishes and fears projected to the group. In this paper, I will focus on the group's role in the development of the elements that ultimately become the building blocks of the individual's identity.

The pull human beings feel towards satisfying the need of belonging to a group has been termed *gregariousness*. We understand that this phenomenon has ethological roots, and resembles behaviors displayed in ants, bees, and other animals as a collective survival mechanism – which may lead to the individual sacrifice in the interest of the colony.

I believe that the same push that enables the child to differentiate from his mother, fostered by the father's presence during the first three years of life (Maher, 1968), will impel him during adolescence to differentiate and separate from his parental figures when encouraged by the group. In other words, the same impulse that spurs the adolescent towards the group and constitutes its gregariousness, is the one that compels the child to achieve individuation and emotional growth.

I should clarify that adolescent gregariousness does not yet imply the mature adult emotional sense of belonging, which culminates in a judicious loyalty to group and country. In adolescence, gregariousness is observed in various stages of evolution.

Group identity is the product of a collective effort, reached through group phenomena that allow the synthesis of its various components. It is thus that a club, school, association, and – certainly – a nation are to develop their own identity. This structure derives from the synthesis of each member's own group identity and, as such, it contains diverse substructures. Some of these are both objective and subjective representations of national identity, and others are simply affective elements encased in the term patriotism.

A country develops its own identity through a process of synthesis that implies the collective mental activity, and the neutralization of ambivalent affects set in motion along the process. Due to the nature of this phenomenon, the development of national identity can be best described as an adolescent group phenomenon.

Just as in individual adolescence, in a national adolescence several contradictory elements of identity that have not yet melded coexist. This joint existence is possible through the use of defense mechanisms such as splitting and denial. And just as in individual adolescence, the national one moves towards a unified identity, solid convictions, and a consistent character that is predictable and reliable. Ultimately, this sets the country on a potential path of productivity.

By contrast, an unresolved national adolescence – like the individual one – results in an ambivalent and contradictory identity that hesitates in its values, exhibits unpredictability that provokes mistrust, and has an erratic and inconsistent productivity.

All nations undergo this adolescent process; its complications are in direct proportion to the degree of ambivalence towards its elements of identity. Those ambivalent elements coexist and are exhibited at times, and at other moments are split and denied. Those nations with multiple and conflictive cultural, ethnic, and religious origins will have a tumultuous adolescence.

During the process of synthesis of the Mexican national identity there have been multiple elements very difficult to process; therefore, they remain active through contradiction, denial, or splitting. These elements originated from the convergence of traumatic events resulting from the interaction of diverse ethnic groups.

In the next chapters, I will address the following main contradictory elements:

1) The fact that Spanish *conquistadores* (conquerors) subdued and destroyed the Aztec Empire. This provoked negative identity figures.

2) The justifications used by the Spaniards to rationalize the aforementioned destruction.

3) The denigration and devaluation of indigenous elements during colonial times. These attitudes were fed by the *criollo*[1] and *mestizo*[2] groups and lasted well into post-independent times.

4) The hatred and disavowal of Spanish elements during and after the Independence Movement conveniently incited by both the *criollo* and *mestizo* groups, which invested the *peninsulares*[3] with every undesirable attribute, while splitting themselves off from this group.

Just as in individual adolescence, each of these conflict-generating factors feeds off of each other and of themselves.

---

[1] *Criollo* is the child born in Mexico to Spaniard parents.

[2] *Mestizo* is the offspring of a Spaniard and a native.

[3] *Peninsular* was the name given to those Spaniards born in Spain, but who lived in Mexico.

6

2

CONQUEST AND DESTRUCTION OF THE AZTEC EMPIRE

With regard to the first factor, it is clear that the *conquistadores'* main mission was to eradicate all language, religion, and architecture they encountered in the New World. Naturally, this also included the elimination of all ideology and art linked to them, as well as of anyone who interfered with this undertaking. The *peninsulares'* strategy in what was to become New Spain was to take advantage of the hatred the Tlaxcaltecas[4] and other neighboring tribes felt towards the Aztecs, who had subjugated all the inhabitants of the region. Once Tenochtitlán[5] fell, however, all these other tribes were equally subjugated by the Spaniards. Several authors have estimated that in 1521, the autochthonous population of New

---

[4] Tlaxcala (Site of the Corn Tortillas) was a neighboring enemy kingdom of the Aztec Empire.

[5] The capital of the Aztec Empire.

Spain was somewhere between nine and twenty-five million. Just a century and a half later, this had fallen to barely over one-and-a-half million.[6] The war of conquest and ensuing poverty had an initial role in this; but the main cause for the dramatic reduction of the indigenous population was the innate vulnerability the natives had for illnesses to which the Spaniards were immune, and which they and the black slaves they imported had brought along.

Fray Toribio de Benavente (a Franciscan missionary) describes one African slave amongst many who was "ill with the pox" and thus introduced smallpox to the colonies. Benavente went on to describe how families and then entire populations were decimated. The natives watched with awed hopelessness how their relatives perished by the hundreds, and how prayers to their gods went unacknowledged. By contrast – the irony of immunity – they thought the gods and goddesses of the white people were protecting them effectively from this disease. In the end, as a result of the apocalypse, there were far fewer natives left than what many wanted to believe.

After the *conquistadores*, a new type of Spaniards arrived in the New Spain. These were priests, missionaries, noblemen (lower nobility), veterans of the Middle Eastern conflicts (who, bored in Spain, had come in search of adventure), artisans, merchants, and shopkeepers. Nevertheless, by far,

---

[6] Lerner, Victoria (1968). Consideraciones sobre la población de la Nueva España: 1793-1810, según Humboldt y Navarro y Noriega. México: Colegio de México.

the largest group that came by the thousands was comprised of adventurers, gamblers, vagabonds, and general riffraff. It is said that by 1560 there were over sixty thousand *peninsulares*. Spaniards continued to flock to America, so much so that the populations of Spanish cities like Burgos (the Cid's hometown) were in alarming descent. This mass migration to New Spain did not ease up until the 18ᵗʰ century.

Slavery wreaked havoc during the 16ᵗʰ century even though the Spanish king had forbidden enslavement of the natives since 1530. The *Encomienda*,[7] a feudal form of exploitation, was officially eradicated by the King in 1542; in reality, it persisted in the New Spain until the beginning of the following century. The *Tiendas de Raya*,[8] an invention of Fray Bartolomé De Las Casas (Spanish colonist turned Dominican friar), substituted slavery, and kept the natives in debt and captive in their jobs. If any attempted to escape, they were promptly returned to their master. De Las Casas, ever so merciful towards the mistreated and exploited natives, proposed the importation of black slaves instead.

The second- and third-rate Spaniards perfected and perpetuated the use of bribery and kickbacks to bureaucrats to keep them efficient and to prevent their files from being

---

[7] *Encomienda* – from the Spanish "to entrust", was a grant by the Crown to a *conquistador*, soldier, official, or others, of a specified number of natives living in a particular area. In exchange for protection and teaching of the Catholic faith, the natives were asked for a tribute in gold or labor.

[8] A *Tienda de Raya* was a company store, owned by the employer. Low level employees, workers, and farmers would be paid in coupons that could be exchanged for goods in these stores.

accidentally "misplaced". The *tortuguista*[9] bureaucracy and corruption were rampant both in New Spain as well as in Spain. Government posts were practically auctioned and were passed down within families. The higher posts were sold in Spain, while the lesser ones, in Mexico. The viceroys were directly appointed by the Spanish king and had a six-year term on average. The vast majority would become extremely wealthy during their *sexenio*.[10]

It was unavoidable then, that Spanish figures with negative connotations were created. The *conquistadores*, the slave traders, the exploiters, and the *encomenderos* (those in charge of the *encomiendas*) were to generate the hatred and disavowal that fueled the insurgence of the Independence Movement.

Thus, the Mexican people – as is sometimes acknowledged – come essentially from the encounter of two cultures. In truth, this encounter was brutal and bloody. Muralist Jorge González Camarena dramatically depicted this cruel encounter in his mural *Fusión de Dos Culturas (The Fusion of Two Cultures)*.

---

[9] From the Spanish *tortuga* (tortoise). Meaning that moves at a tortoise's pace.

[10] *Sexenio* is popularly used to refer to a Mexican presidential term, which lasts six years. The author hereby draws a parallel between viceroys and current Mexican presidents (Translator's Note).

This allegory has been reproduced on the reverse of the fifty-thousand-peso bill.

On the obverse – the proverbial flipside – there is an image of Cuauhtémoc (the last Aztec Emperor).

Another of González Camarena's murals, *El Abrazo* (*The Hug*) strongly underscores both the ironic and catastrophic nature of the encounter.

Former president, José López Portillo (1976-1982) declared in the summer of 1992 that the discovery of America constituted a "cosmic catastrophe to the autochthonous races, whereby gods became demons; kings, slaves; and slaves, dust".

3

JUSTIFICATION FOR THE DESTRUCTION

With regard to the second element – the justification – as mental health professionals, we cannot deny the intrinsic value of a rationalization. In fact, we can reason that the *conquistadores* had a set of moral values and religious convictions, as well as loyalty towards their king and country. After all, these values had nourished their own Spanish national identity. Nevertheless, also as observers of human behavior, we know that mankind is not always motivated by its love of others, God, or religion. Humans are compelled by their quest to return to the omnipotence experienced during their symbiotic relationship early in childhood with their mother (Mahler, 1968). Narcissism and lust for power is what ultimately drove Alexander the Great, Nebuchadnezzar, Julius Cesar, Genghis Khan, Tiberius and Titus; Catholic Queen Isabella, Cortés, Pizarro, Balboa, and Alvarado. History shows us how malignant narcissism flourished in these historical figures, who even resorted to murdering their rivals in their quest for power.

Selfishness, greed, and lust for power hid behind religion and, thus found its justification for the conquest as means to evangelize the pagans. After all, the same motive had been used to justify the massacres in times of Pelayo, the Cid, and – later on – during the siege of Moorish Granada. When Granada fell to the rule of Castile and Aragon, mere months before Columbus had arrived in the New World, thousands of moors perished in the fierce and bloody battle. Women were defiled, and their daughters sold in public auction. This earned Ferdinand and Isabella the title of Catholic Monarchs, granted by the Spanish Pope, Alexander VI – the Borgia pope. Furthermore, the later massacres of Cholula, Puebla, and Tenochtitlán brought Isabella close to beatification.

When Fray Servando Teresa de Mier[11] questioned whether the love for the Cross and the desire to redeem the souls of the infidels had been the sole motivation for the conquest, he was nearly accused of heresy. He also expressed that Christianity itself had not been brought by the Spaniards; rather, by St. Thomas Apostle, known in the New World as *Quetzalcóatl.*[12] Furthermore, he preached that the Virgin of Tepeyac[13] was known even before the conquest as *Tonantzin,* and that her image had been drawn not on Juan Diego's

---

[11] Mexican Catholic priest and politician (1765-1827).

[12] The main deity of Mesoamerican cultures whose name means "feathered serpent" in Náhuatl. Quetzalcóatl was considered by the Aztecs the creator of life.

[13] Also known as the Virgin of Guadalupe, patron saint of Mexico.

cloak[14], but on Quetzalcóatl's cape (or St. Thomas, rather). In truth, by making these declarations, in an attempt to destroy anything remotely Spanish, he stepped over the line. Mier became the prototype of a *criollo* and then of a Mexican – splitting and denying his own heritage – just like Lucas Alamán[15] became the archetypal pro-Spanish Mexican – the other side of the split.

With regard to religion and language, the justification was that the natives were pagan savages. Anything indigenous had to be denigrated and despised. This notion presupposed that only the natives, and not the Spaniards, had to be transformed; and that their culture, art, religion, and language had no value. Consequently, it exaggerated the value of what *peninsulares* brought with them to the New World, and diminished the value of what they took back to Spain. This caused a polarization, in which anything Spanish was rejected and split from the self-perception. One perfect example of this posture was Lucas Alamán's who, as mentioned before, was loyal to the Spanish Crown. His own hispanophilia stoked the extreme anti-Spanish sentiment seen in Fray Servando Teresa de Mier. In turn, Mier's denigration of anything Spanish caused an anti-American movement in Europe. And thus, the vicious circle of denigration and lack of synthesis was perpetuated.

---

[14] Official Catholic accounts state that in 1531 Our Lady of Guadalupe appeared to a native peasant, Juan Diego, on the Hill of Tepeyac, in what later became the suburbs of modern Mexico City.

[15] Lucas Alamán (1792-1853), conservative Mexican politician and intellectual, loyal to the Spanish Crown.

16

4

DENIGRATION OF NATIVE ASPECTS

To understand this third element preventing a complete synthesis of national identity, we should pause to reflect that at the time of the War of Independence (1810) there were about one million *criollos* in New Spain. During the colonial times they were called Spaniards and comprised 20% of the population. Another 20% was made up of *mestizos*, and three more million were natives. There were only a few tens of thousands *peninsulares* (also called *gachupines*[16]) as well as the descendants of the more than two hundred and fifty thousand black slaves imported during three centuries of colony. The *criollos*, depending on their social ranking, had two, three, or more native – and even an occasional black – mistresses, aside from their wives in their palatial haciendas. These mistresses, along with their respective *chilpayates* and *pipiltotontin*,[17] lived in little huts on the periphery of the hacien-

---

[16] *Gachupín* comes from the Náhuatl *catzopini*, or "man with spurs" or "man on horse". It is used to refer to a Spanish settler in America who immigrated from Spain.

[17] The Náhuatl words for children and adolescents.

da, which became known as the *"casas chicas"* (small houses). Those legitimate *mestizos* (the offspring of a marriage between a peninsular and a native, or a *criollo* and a native or a *criollo* and a *mestizo*) made it a point to identify themselves as Spaniards (*criollos*). Those born of illegitimate unions had to be inscribed in the *Infamy Registry* of their local parishes. Since the marriages between a black person – or its descendant – and a *criollo* or a peninsular were not recognized under the law, all their offspring were labeled "negorid" (*mulatto, cambujo, zambo, barcino, coyote* and *albarazado*[18]), and were automatically inscribed in the same registry. Natives could only perform the lowliest work and were considered minors under the law throughout their entire life. In other words, they were regarded as mentally retarded.

During colonial times most *mestizos* and *criollos* identified themselves as *peninsulares* – the dominant group – and went to great lengths to conceal any dissimilarity. In that broad sense, children born to any other group were considered bastards and were thus entered in the Infamy Registry. Therefore, everyone with any Spanish connection had to boast about it. The discrimination against anything not Spanish, and particularly anything native, split these elements of identification and to this day remain difficult to reincorporate.

---

[18] Mulatto: mix between African and European; *cambujo*: mix between black and native; *zambo*: mix between African and native; *barcino*: mix between *lobo* (Chinese-native and mulatto) and Chinese; *albarazado*: mix between *gíbaro* (*lobo* and mulatto) and mulatto; *coyote*: mix between native and *mestizo*.

5

DISAVOWAL OF SPANISH ELEMENTS

Finally, the fourth element interfering with a cohesive national identity, and which led to the independence movement, derived from the need to shrug off all Spanish elements and place them exclusively on the *peninsulares*. There, these elements were attacked in the hopes of permanently erasing them from the nascent Mexican identity. When these different parts were hidden – denied – they became compartmentalized; therefore, the Mexican identity remained only partially complete.[19] Humboldt described that around the time of the

---

[19] I identify here the utilization of a defense mechanism that consists on the projection of undesirable elements upon an object, which is then attacked, destroyed, or excluded. The projection object has the characteristics which are to be repudiated, thus it is conveniently chosen. The illusion the subject creates is one of having rid himself entirely of these characteristics. I shall refer to this subterfuge as the *mechanism of convenient extinction*, with the understanding that it results from the workings of other mechanisms, like projection. This *mechanism of convenient extinction* occurs frequently during adolescence.

Independence Movement, only the *criollos* living in the outer provinces called themselves Spaniards. Those living in major cities, especially Mexico City, did not want to be considered as such. They called themselves *American*, and made all efforts to distinguish themselves from the white citizens born in Spain, who were now dubbed *gachupines*. This is probably the time when this description first acquired its pejorative meaning. Up until then, the word was commonly used, even in documents issued by the vice-regal government.

The Independence Movement was sparked by the disagreement between Spain and the *criollos* regarding the heavy tax burdens consequence of the Peninsular War, which was a war between Spain and France. It should be noted that this fiscal duty fell entirely upon the *criollos*, since the natives did not pay taxes – they only paid a modest yearly tribute of two pesos per family. A struggle between the so-called insurgents and the royalists ensued. Spaniards, *mestizos,* and *criollos* took sides – and some took both sides. The natives were used as cannon fodder, just as during the *Conquista* (conquest). They had no military training, as they were exempt from military duty and were forbidden from horseback ridding.

At one point, in 1808, since New Spain declared the Spanish government illegitimate, the proclamation of an independent government with Viceroy José de Iturrigaray (a *peninsular*) as king was briefly conspired. In the end, he was removed and later accused of treason. Miguel Domínguez, Mayor of the City of Querétaro at the time and collaborator of this conspiracy, helped destroy all incriminating evidence against Iturrigaray. Shortly after, though, the famous literary meetings that routinely took place in his home (hosted by his wife, Doña Josefa Ortiz) became insurgent ones.

During the 18th century, the Spaniards – meaning *peninsulares* and *criollos* – had exploited the natives. After the Independence, the *criollos* became the sole abusers; though they blamed the *peninsulares* for all the excesses, casting themselves as the saviors of the natives. However, after three centuries, the art of smooth-talking – popular since the times of Fray Bartolomé – began to lose its effect. The natives rebelled, some quite forcibly. In Sonora, the Yaqui tribe attacked *criollos* and *mestizos* alike. In Yucatan, in July 1847, the last Maya effort to recover freedom and dominion of their land was launched. One of such plots was discovered by the government: The Mayas were planning to behead all whites and *mestizos* just as the blacks in Haiti did to the French. As a result, some Mayan leaders faced the firing squad. Under the assumption that many other coconspirators had escaped, government forces set the town of Tepich on fire, preventing women, children, and the elderly to flee their homes. This became known as the War of the Castes of the Yucatan peninsula; it lasted fifty-four years. Yet the inequality issues that led to it continued until 1937.

Ms. Rigoberta Menchú still warns that the inequality remains, and the threat of armed uprisings is still very real. Her parents and siblings were murdered, and her people (the Quiche, not the Guatemalan) have been subject to many violations and injustices. Rigoberta even had to learn Spanish to make herself be heard. Her outcry was so loud it reached the other side of the Atlantic Ocean. Around our neck of the woods, most had not heard a peep.[20]

---

[20] Rigoberta Menchú was awarded the Nobel Peace Prize on October 16, 1992.

6

CURRENT ATTEMPTS AT INTEGRATION

Five hundred years since the first encounter and after more than 180 years of independence, there are about two million families in Mexico of indigenous roots living in the most relegated communities of Mexican society. There are some, like former President López Portillo, who think this is due to their marginalization; others believe it is idiosyncratic. The combined efforts of the government and a large and expensive group of experts to reach the cultural integration of native communities have yielded poor results.

By the way, during the October 12, 1992 protests, at least three different phenomena were observed. There were the groups of natives that show up every year to march toward the Basilica of Guadalupe, the La Raza Monument (the monument to honor Mexican ethnicity), and the Columbus Monument. However, since 1992 marked the five-hundredth anniversary of Colon's arrival, these protests actually made the news. The second type of march was comprised of people who damaged these same monuments. This also occurred in numerous cities throughout the American continent. Amongst the vandal groups there were youngsters who sported extravagant clothes and hair styles, referred to as "punks" by the press. Finally, there were radical so-called indigenist groups that demanded a total secession from the whites, and a change in official language. They even made animal sacrifices at the Basilica's atrium. Had they obtained the proper permits, they might have performed human sacrifices instead!

I understand that there is legitimacy to some of the natives' protests. However, I also believe there is opportunism to attack the establishment. There is also evidence of ambivalence and hostility toward the Spanish elements of the Mexican people; these elements are hated, projected, split and attacked.[21] The caption of a photograph in a major newspaper read: "Radical indigenous groups that repudiate the history of America, converged at the main square to express their inconformity with what they are: mestizos, children of two races, but a distinct and unique one." I don't know if this monstrosity of a caption was a *lapsus calami* or an irony. Local authorities made sure that all damages were repaired by the end of the day. Just like everything else in Mexico – even death – these events ended up as the butt of jokes. The conflict remained in suspense, waiting for a better opportunity to be processed.

---

[21] Which, as I mentioned before, I have labeled *mechanism of convenient extinction.*

7

EL CABALLITO

In 1992, Mexico had only had 182 years of independent life. These were preceded by three hundred years of colonial rule during which many different elements of identity were forged. The melting pot contained multiple identity ingredients: The Spanish medieval and Renaissance, the Visigoth, the Arabic, and the Jewish; all of which blended with the Náhuatl ones. Ambivalence was set in motion, and these contradicting elements coexisted, but without arriving at a synthesis.

After the War of Independence there have been several instances illustrating this ambivalence toward the contradicting elements. One is the story and fate of the equestrian monument of the Spanish king Charles IV (1788-1819).

This singular sculpture is undoubtedly a magnificent work of art, and has a spectacular size. It is the only statue of its kind founded from one single mold. It was created by the Spanish architect Manuel Tolsá, who bequeathed to the New Spain – and later to independent Mexico – his creativity and teachings as a member of the faculty of the *Academia de San Carlos* art school.

Viceroy Iturrigaray revealed the statue in 1803 at Mexico City's main square. After the Declaration of Independence in 1810, the figure of King Charles IV became the symbol of the loathed colonialism to anti-Spanish Mexicans, like Fray Servando. Conversely, for the pro-Spanish Mexicans, like Lucas Alamán, Charles IV had merely been a clumsy, weak, and womanizing king responsible for the loss of Spain's colonies and of its greatness. However, both groups, independent of each other, recognized Tolsa's grand artistic talent. Emperor

Iturbide[22], unable to deal with either the statue or his own ambivalence, covered it with a blue globelike structure. Guadalupe Victoria[23], a less sensitive man, wanted to melt the statue and turn it into a fence for the *Alameda*.[24] Lucas Alamán (see footnote 15 on page 15) saved the statue from this fate and transported it in 1824 to a secure location: the inner courtyard of the University,[25] then situated next to what is now *Palacio Nacional,* behind the *Plaza del Volador.*[26] The statue's balustrade was sent to the Alameda and its railing to the Chapultepec Castle.

---

[22] Also known as Augustine of Mexico – a Mexican army general who ruled Mexico from 1822 to 1823.

[23] Guadalupe Victoria was Mexico's first elected president from 1824 to 1829.

[24] Mexico's public park in the heart of the city.

[25] The image of Charles IV equestrian statue standing in the courtyard of the Pontifical University of Mexico (which eventually became the National Autonomous University of Mexico – UNAM) was printed in the back of the two-thousand-peso bill, as illustrated.

[26] *Palacio Nacional* is the seat of the Executive Power, and the *Plaza del Volador* is the current location of the Supreme Court.

While at the University, the statue was not exempt from the occasional stoning or having a bucket of paint thrown at it by radical students – who were fortunately not as drastic as those who dynamited the statue of President Miguel Alemán at the National Autonomous University in the 1960's. The Charles IV statue remained in the University until 1852, when the conservative government of Mariano Arista allowed it to peek out.

Later, the statue was moved to the then outer limit of Mexico City, a virtually deserted area except for the bullring and the beginning of Avenida Bucareli.[27] It was during this process that it acquired its ironic-pejorative diminutive "*El Caballito*" (Little Horse), so characteristic of the Spanish language spoken in Mexico. From its new location, *El Caballito* watched Mexico grow, until it became an inconvenience and thus, like the other well-known Mexican statue *La Diana Cazadora* (Diana de Huntress), was taken out of the way.

---

[27] A main avenue that ran east-west toward the historical downtown.

More recently, in 1972, after attempting to rediscover heroes, and pre- and postcolonial values, a new effort was made to recover *criollo* traditions and symbols. An example of this was the issue of the $1000 bank note, which shows the image of the very Spanish Colonial Plaza of Santo Domingo. However, the statue of Mayor Miguel Domínguez' wife (mentioned on page 21) is not depicted, even though in actuality it has been at the square since the early 20th century.

Similarly, the Manuel Tolsá square was named to honor the famous architect and sculptor of *El Caballito;* and despite its plain nature, it is bordered on its south side by Tolsa's *Palacio de Minería*[28], a stunning piece of architecture. In 1972, *El Caballito* was moved to this square, even though it was not as eye-catching as it was in its previous location, where it had become a well-known landmark. Unfortunately, only the pigeons pay attention to it now. It should be noted that the roundabout where the statue once stood remained empty for twenty years. When the statue of *La Diana* was returned to its original location at Paseo de la Reforma, people wondered if *El Caballito* would also go back to its previous site. However, in its stead, a more modern equestrian statue – another *caballito* – was erected, representative of the geometric movement of the 20th century.

---

[28] The Palacio de Minería housed the Royal School of Mining until 1954.

Sometimes, like any good adolescent, Mexican culture imports completely foreign elements of identity. For example, there were Mexican composers who wrote operas in French, since Spanish was deemed too vulgar a language to be used in *bel canto*. At the end of the 19th century, anything French represented elegance. Even architecture became Frenchy. So much so, that several buildings were retrofitted with French façades. Therefore, they were only superficially French, similar to the "as if" phenomenon of adolescence. The best example of this architectural fashion is the parish church of San Miguel de Allende, in Guanajuato. Built during the 18th century in the Spanish style, at the time in which the town was still known as San Miguel el Grande (St. Michael the Great), the church debuted its new gothic façade during the rule of President Porfirio Díaz (1876-1880 and 1884-1911), a century later.

Curiously, the only structure Mexican architects learned to build in the French style were façades, because they copied them from engravings and postcards brought from Europe. Therefore, many other churches were also built with French façades but with Spanish Romance interiors.

History and its ghosts: The Colony, Tolsá, Guadalupe Victoria, Lucas Alamán, conservatives and liberals; even former president López Portillo, Sebastián (the sculptor of the modern *El Caballito*), and San Miguel de Allende witness and linger in our national adolescent history.

8

THE NATIONAL ANTHEM

The history of our National Anthem also exemplifies our ambivalences. It celebrates the deeds of people once considered heroes, but who eventually were solicitously forgotten by history. For example, the fourth stanza was erased because it alluded to the patriotic actions of General Iturbide (who later proclaimed himself Emperor). Later on, the seventh stanza was also eliminated, because it referenced President Santa Anna's heroism. Then, when it became fashionable to boast about Mexican pacifism, it was suggested to suppress all stanzas that had a bellicose tone. Thanks to General Manuel Ávila Camacho's presidential decree of October 20, 1942, all further edits to the Anthem were forbidden. To this date, we only sing four of the original ten stanzas written by an imprudent poet, Francisco González Bocanegra.

González Bocanegra was a Mexican who had once been a *criollo*; in other words, a Spaniard. He was exiled to the Spanish city of Cadiz at the age of five, when his *peninsular* father could no longer avoid the 1827 Mexican law of expulsion of *peninsulares*. Francisco's own ambivalence to enter the Anthem Competition was overcome by his girlfriend, Guadalupe (the source of inspiration to several of his poems). She locked him in his room until, several hours later, he slid the pages with his lyrics back under the door to Guadalupe. González Bocanegra also wrote other great poems, like the "Ode to Miramón", a tribute to a conservative general of the time.

As for the music of the anthem, Spanish musician Jaime Nunó found inspiration in the glorious bell peals of the Mexico City Metropolitan Cathedral. Nunó had used "God and Liberty" as his identifying motto and signed his work with the initials JN. Unaware of the author's identity (as established in the contest rules), the judges determined that his musical piece most closely expressed and exhibited the national pride.

The National Anthem made its debut on May 27, 1854, at the then Teatro Oriente, but not with the music composed by Nunó, a Spaniard, but with that by the Italian Giacomo Bottesini. Then, something happened. Perhaps President Santa Anna himself imposed Nunó's score (he had brought Nunó from Cuba); or perhaps it was agreed that Nunó was really not a Spaniard but a Catalan. In the end, Nunó's version of the National Anthem was played on September 15, 1854, at the Santa Anna Theater, with Bottesini as conductor. González Bocanegra gave the introductory remarks. Yet, President Santa Anna – who by then had declared himself dictator for life with the title "Most Serene Highness" – did not appear.

The event was not noted in the Federal Official Gazette. Nunó and González Bocanegra never received the awards they had won, yet their anthem surpassed all others, and Mexicans consider it the most beautiful anthem in the world – of course, second only to *La Marseillese*!

President Santa Anna, who apparently had a thing for contests, had promoted another one in 1843 for the construction of a monument to Independence, to be placed on the main square of Mexico City. The winner this time was also a Spaniard: Lorenzo de la Hidalga, who had constructed the Volador Market and the National Theater. Nevertheless, the monument in question was never built, only the plinth where it would have stood. With time, the word *Zócalo* (Spanish for plinth) became synonymous in Mexico with Main Square. The *Zócalo* was later officially named Plaza de la Constitución (Constitution Square), referring to the 1917 Constitution. Of note, the square had already been designated *Constitution Square* before, in 1813, after the Cadiz Constitution had been signed in 1812 by Viceroy Calleja.

A few years later, the authorities lost the sheet music to the National Anthem. Praise be to Freud! It was not until the 20th century that a commission of several personalities was charged with the recovery and rediscovery of the National Anthem. Among its members were Jose López Portillo and German-trained musicologist, Professor Julián Carrillo. López Portillo's grandson and namesake would rediscover Quetzalcóatl and become President of Mexico. Carrillo rediscovered the "Thirteenth Sound", a musical theory lost since the Middle Ages that recognized thirteen tones in an octave instead of the twelve currently accepted. During the commission's work, our anthem lost its march tempo and its bass and baritone undertones.

In 1953, the centennial year of the anthem, yet another contest was convened (this time not by Santa Anna!) to pick four designs for commemorative stamps. Three out of the four winner drawings were created by a Spanish refugee painter – José Renau.

9

THE VIRGIN OF GUADALUPE

Fray Servando Teresa de Mier (see footnote [11] on page 14) used to say, "Everything in America is different, colors seem different." "Language sounds different; it has become softer... Even the dogs brought by the *peninsulares* ceased to bark when they encountered the *xoloitzcuintli* (Aztec dogs)", Henestrosa said.[29] The gods also changed. Syncretism took care of this in a natural way. As in many other parts of the world, pagan temples were demolished and churches were built in their place. Frequently, though, the natives continued to worship their own idols, which they secretly placed in hidden spots behind or underneath Christian images. Spanish priests, when speaking Náhuatl, used the name *Tonantzin* when referring to the Virgin Mary. Tonantzin means "Our Mother", name given by the natives to the mother of all the

---

[29] Professor Andrés Henestrosa: Conference titled "Encounter of Two Worlds. Five hundred years after the American Conquest." The Medical Society of the American British Cowdray Hospital, Mexico City, October 22, 1992.

gods. She had her own temple, built before the *Conquista* at the Cerro del Tepeyac.[30] It was said that the goddess appeared in a youthful form to reveal secrets, always to one native at a time. This was not the only ideological superimposition: Christ's inherent goodness caused him to be frequently mistaken for Quetzalcóatl. Other times, he was confused for Huitzilopochtli because – according to Aztec belief – his mother Coatlicue conceived him without any physical contact with a man. Huitzilopochtli, the war god, was also confused for St. James Apostle, given his warrior attributes. While Saint Isidore (patron saint of farmers) was mistaken for Tláloc (the god of the rain, drought and agriculture).

---

[30] The Tepeyac Hill is the current site of the Basilica of Our Lady of Guadalupe.

During colonial times, the Virgin of Guadalupe was perceived, through splitting, as having at least three different identities. To the natives, she was the *Indita* (the little native girl); to the *criollos*, the *Criollita* (little *criolla*), and to the *mestizos*, the *Mesticita* (little *mestiza*). The Spaniards had the Virgin of los Remedios (the Virgin Mary to the Trinitarian order), dubbed the *Gachupina*. She was claimed to have saved the Spanish army during their flight to Popotla after the battle that culminated in the famous *Noche Triste*.[31] The *Gachupina* had purportedly distracted the Aztecs, allowing the Spaniards to flee. During the War of Independence, there was a generalized dislike for the Virgin of Los Remedios. When her penchant fell under enemy forces, it would be defiled. Conversely, the royalists would do the same to the *Guadalupana* penchant. During those times, in the split, each part had its own deities.

---

[31] On June 30, 1520, Hernán Cortés' army and its allied non-Aztec native combatants lost a mayor battle to the Aztecs. This became known as The Night of Sorrows, or *Noche Triste*. Cortés had kidnapped Aztec Emperor Montezuma II and tortured him until he ordered his people to surrender. Other Aztec leaders discovered the scheme and unleashed the Aztec army, which was finally defeated by Cortés in the Battle of Otumba, two weeks later.

10

OUR CONTEMPORARY MEXICO

Just as there was a quest for saints during colonial times, throughout our history there has been a search for heroes, identification figures to cement national sentiment. In 1949, Professor Eulalia Guzmán discovered, hidden in the ruins of a church in Ixcateopan, Guerrero, what she believed to be the remains of Cuauhtémoc, the last Aztec emperor (see page 11). The government at that time, less strict than Archbishop Zumárraga,[32] declared the church a national landmark. The remains found by Eulalia Guzmán still lie in that church.

In the national adolescent process in which we live, we sometimes launch fireworks on the eve of Independence Day (September 15), without realizing we are celebrating St. Porfirio.[33] We have hidden, in a cunning way, idols behind images

---

[32] Fray Juan de Zumárraga, the first Archbishop of Mexico City from 1530 to 1548, would have considered this idolatry.

[33] President Porfirio Díaz used the celebration of his birthday and saint day, which is on September 15, to commence the Independence Day festivities. This has remained the tradition since; although, the actual Independence Day is September 16.

we supposedly worship. No matter how "white" we are, we cannot help sometimes feel as native as President Benito Juárez (a member of the Zapoteco tribe) or even as Cuauhtémoc, the last Aztec Emperor. No matter how far we are from the ideal Hispanic, there is always someone more crass, more vulgar, or more *naco*[34] to despise.

The split identifications of Hispanic nations – ours – allow the *neocriollo* to deny his Spanish origins (like it occurred 200 years ago), boast his native roots and yet, despise anything indigenous. Just as 200 years ago, we – the *neocriollos* – seem to continue to minimize the differences between ones and the others. We all fall under the same demonym but, whenever possible, we tend to take advantage of any privileged position. We brag about our social contacts and influences (long live the *neocriollos*!), and let the natives and mediocre be the ones who wait in line.

Present-day Mexicans, whichever their foreign ancestry might be – Spanish, German, Saxon, or Hebrew – should continue along the adolescent path towards synthesis, which allows the existence of their other ancestry, inherited from the Aztecs. Those Mexicans with surnames like O'Gorman, Gerzso, Goeritz, Mayer or Meyer may have more elements to integrate but, just like the rest of us, they will still have to struggle with all the contradictions we inherited in our Mexican history. I noted this on an 8-year-old patient with blond hair, blue eyes, and milky-white skin, whose last name ended

---

[34] Mexican slang to describe the bad-mannered, poorly educated people, or those with bad taste.

in 'ansky'. It was September 14, and it had coincided with Yom Kippur. With a sweet voice he said, "Tomorrow is also the day when we defeated the Spaniards."

Coppery skin that envies whiteness with nostalgia; pale-looking skin that longs for darkening. Language, religion, architecture, drama, poetry, agriculture… all should have hybridized to sculpt the new nations. Recent celebrities claim dubious ancestry; ambivalence towards Spanish things coexists with an ambiguous indigenism. Amphibological lineage from a chaotic heritage… A society in constant effort that, even after 500 years, continues to struggle for the synthesis of elements at odds with each other. An identity still in process that ignores and fails to recognize the elements that shape it. Peoples who fight for synthesis in their quest for individuation, by using mechanisms that generate an "as if" persona, thus creating myths. Peoples who alter the history of their ancestors, just like the teenager who – cringing at the possibility of resembling his parents – rebels, pretending to have nothing to do with them. Only to repeat their story.

The same North Star – Polaris – that still shines in the north and guided Columbus in his journey, also guided the architects of Tenochtitlán. Tonantzin, disguised as the Virgin of Guadalupe in the Tepeyac is revered in the Americas, just as much as President Benito Juárez.

Lorca said, "Who will come? And where from? Big hoarfrost stars/come with the fish of shadow/that opens the road of dawn." Those false prophets gave us the promise that *bringeth* not the last word. We still await the arrival of synthesis, ordered by the "Lord of what is near and beside", as foretold by Quetzalcóatl. Let those who come from our mysterious inside arrive. Let them show us the quests given to Axayácatl and Tezozómoc by Netzahualcóyotl,[35] when he spoke to them about love. Yet, let the quests open our eyes and hearts, and teach us how to sing well, burn the ships, and look ahead...

---

[35] Tezozómoc was ruler of the city-state Azcapotzalco (c. 1370-1426). Axayácatl was the ruler of the Aztec Triple Alliance (1469-1481). Nezahaulcóyotl was the ruler of the city-state Texcoco (1429-1472). He was also a philosopher, architect, and poet. Nezahualcóyotl famously used his wisdom to mediate peace – as a young man – with Tezozómoc and – as an old man – with Axayácatl.

REFERENCES

Freud, S. (1930): El malestar en la cultura. *Obras Completas*, 3:1-65. Madrid: Editorial Biblioteca Nueva.

Fromm, E. (1947): *Man for Himself*. Greenwich, CT: Fawcett Publications.

Blos, P. (1962): *On Adolescence: A Psychoanalytic Interpretation*. New York: Free Press of Glencoe.

López, M. I. (1990): *La Encrucijada de la Adolescencia*. México: Hispánicas.

Mahler, M. (1968): *On Human Symbiosis and the Vicissitudes of Individuation. I: Infantile Psychosis*. Nueva York: IUP.

48

ABOUT THE AUTHOR

Manuel Isaías López, MD, PhD graduated from the Mexican National Autonomous University (UNAM) School of Medicine, specialized in Adult and in Child and Adolescent Psychiatry at the Medical College of Pennsylvania. He graduated as a psychoanalyst and child psychoanalyst and was a training and supervising analyst at the Mexican Institute of Psychoanalysis of the Mexican Psychoanalytic Association (APM). He obtained his doctorate degree in Bioethics from the Anáhuac University. Manuel Isaías López authored over 150 original articles on psychiatry, child psychiatry and bioethics, which were published across numerous scientific publications and specialty textbooks. He was Board Certified in Adult and Child and Adolescent Psychiatry by the Mexican Council of Psychiatry, an institution where he was member of the board for twenty years. He was founding member and coordinator for twenty-five years of the Child and Adolescent Psychiatry training program at the Department of Psychiatry of the UNAM School of Medicine. Dr. López was professor of the Masters course in Psychotherapy at the Anáhuac University School of Psychology, and of the Bioethics doctorate program at the Bioethics Department of the Anáhuac University. He was president of the APM, Founding president of the Mexican Association of Child and Adolescent Psychiatry (AMPI); member of the Mexican Psychiatric Association, the Mexican Society of Neurology and Psychiatry, and the American Psychiatric Association; lifetime member of the Mexican Academy of Pediatrics, the American College of Psychiatrists, the American Academy of Child and Adolescent Psychiatry, and the International Psychoanalytical Association. During his last years, he was a member of the Institute for Psychoanalytic Training and Research (IPTAR) in New York City. Aside from various institutional positions, Dr. López also had a private practice in psychiatry, child and adolescent psychiatry, and psychoanalysis for forty-five years.